STUDY GUIDE

D1132677

TRIBULATION

BEGUN?

AMIR TSARFATI

HARVEST PROPHECY
AN IMPRINT OF HARVEST HOUSE PUBLISHERS

All Scripture quotations are taken from the New King James Version®. Copyright © 1982 by Thomas Nelson, Inc. Used by permission. All rights reserved.

Cover design by Bryce Williamson

Cover photo © 4khz, Elena_Garder / Getty Images

Interior design by KUHN Design Group

For bulk, special sales, or ministry purchases, please call 1-800-547-8979. Email: Customerservice@hhpbooks.com

This logo is a federally registered trademark of the Hawkins Children's LLC. Harvest House Publishers, Inc., is the exclusive licensee of this trademark.

Has the Tribulation Begun? Study Guide
Copyright © 2023 by Amir Tsarfati
Published by Harvest House Publishers
Eugene, Oregon 97408
www.harvesthousepublishers.com

ISBN 978-0-7369-8728-8 (pbk)
ISBN 978-0-7369-8729-5 (eBook)

Printed in the United States of America

23 24 25 26 27 28 29 30 31 / BP / 10 9 8 7 6 5 4 3 2 1

CONTENTS

1

HAS THE TRIBULATION BEGUN?

The tribulation is no small event. In the grand panorama of human history, it will last a short seven years. But its impact will be unprecedented.

Revelation 3:10 tells us this "hour of trial…shall come upon the whole world." Isaiah 24:1 says of this time, "Behold, the LORD makes the earth empty and makes it waste, distorts its surface and scatters abroad its inhabitants."

The tribulation will be cataclysmic to a degree we cannot even imagine. That alone makes some people reluctant to learn about it. Others ask, "If all believers are going to be raptured beforehand, there's no real reason for us to be concerned about it, right?"

But because God gave us so much information about the tribulation in the Bible, we can be certain that He wants us to understand what will happen, and why. The Old Testament prophets spoke about it. Shortly before His crucifixion, Jesus gave His disciples a lengthy preview of what would happen. Additional insights are given in some of the epistles. And the book of Revelation devotes a lot of attention to it. There are reasons God wants us to know this information.

Here's why: What the Bible says about the end times isn't meant to merely inform us, but to shape how we live. Look at what Hebrews 10:24-25 says about what we're to do as the end times draw nearer: "Let us consider one another in order to stir up love and good works...exhorting one another, and so much the more as you see the Day approaching."

Our awareness of the coming tribulation is also meant to keep us focused on our mission. Jesus said, "Go therefore and make disciples of all nations" (Matthew 28:19). We're here to point others to salvation in Christ while there is still time.

Yes, the tribulation will be horrific. But God has definite purposes for it, and we should know what they are. As 2 Timothy 3:16-17 says, "All Scripture is given by inspiration of God, and is profitable...that the man of God may be complete, thoroughly equipped for every good work." This includes what the Bible says about the tribulation.

With that in mind, let's learn what we can about the tribulation, and explore the ways it is relevant to both our present and our future.

"When you are done with this book, I want you to be able to do the exact same thing with your loved ones, your friends, your fellow church members—anyone who needs to be comforted with the truth. My goal is for you to be equipped to be able to explain to anyone why this cannot possibly be the tribulation, how they can know the signs that the actual tribulation has begun, and how they can ensure that they won't be around to experience it."

Has the Tribulation Begun?, page 9

IT'S NOT SO BAD

Romans 8:18 says, "I consider that the sufferings of this present time are not worthy to be compared with the glory which shall be revealed in us."

What are some of the sufferings we encounter in life?

What are some of the glorious wonders we can look forward to in our heavenly future?

How do the joys that we anticipate in the future help give us perspective for the problems we face today?

THE SCRIPTURES AND THE POWER OF GOD

When people are confused about an issue addressed in the Bible, often it's because of biblical illiteracy. This was demonstrated by Jesus when the Sadducees challenged Him, asking a question about the resurrection. Jesus gave them a simple answer that proved there is life after death.

Based on your own experience, what are two or three examples of confusion you've seen caused by people not knowing what the Bible says?

What example or two can you give of deception that can easily occur when people don't know their Bibles very well?

Why do you think people are highly vulnerable to deception when it comes to matters that relate to the end times?

As mentioned on page 13 in *Has the Tribulation Begun?*, what is the danger of going from "What does the Bible say?" to "What does the Bible really say?"

TRUTHS BEING TARGETED BY SATAN

Satan's goal has always been to mislead and deceive people about the truth. If he can get them to believe falsehoods, then he can keep them from God, salvation, and a clear understanding of what's really happening in this world. Let's look at some of the truths that Satan attacks.

Targeted Truth 1: Jesus alone is the Life, the Truth, and the Way to God.

In John 14:6, Jesus said, "I am the way, the truth, and the life. No one comes to the Father except through Me." Does Jesus leave any room for exceptions in this statement?

Why is it dangerous for us to diminish, in any way, what Jesus said about the sole means of access to God?

Some people characterize Jesus' words in John 14:6 as being strict and unloving. But why are His words actually the most compassionate statement He could possibly make about salvation and getting to heaven?

Targeted Truth 2: All people are born sinners.

What important fact does Romans 5:12 teach about the origin of sin?

What reality does Romans 3:10-11 communicate about all people?

There are some who believe that if their good works outweigh their bad works, then God will let them into heaven. What Scripture passages would you share with them to help correct their thinking?

Targeted Truth 3: Israel is still God's chosen people and can't be replaced.

Some people believe that because of Israel's frequent rejection of God over such a long period of time, they are no longer His chosen people and have been replaced by the church. But what did the apostle Paul say about God and the Jewish people in Romans 11:1?

When will the partial blindness of Israel end, according to Romans 11:25?

What does Romans 11:26 say will happen after that? Would this serve as evidence that Israel still has a place in God's plans?

What very clear statement does Paul make about God's promises in Romans 11:29?

*Targeted Truth 4: In order to be prepared,
we must know the times and the seasons.*

Bible prophecy reveals how everything will turn out in the end. With that in mind, why do you think Satan would want to discourage people from studying prophecy?

Prophecy encourages us to redeem the time, live holy lives, make every day count, and be eager to share the gospel with the lost. In contrast, what effects might a *lack* of interest in prophecy have on a believer's life?

*Targeted Truth 5: When Jesus returns, we need
to be found doing the Father's business.*

In Luke 12:37, Jesus said, "Blessed are those servants whom the master, when he comes, will find watching."

Scripture does not reveal when the rapture will take place, nor do we know when the tribulation will begin. Why do you think the Lord intentionally chose *not* to provide this information?

In the parable of the minas, before a nobleman departed for a far land, he "called ten of his servants, delivered to them ten minas, and said to them, 'Do business till I come'" (Luke 19:13). Through this parable, Jesus was teaching that we are to stay busy doing His work while we await His coming. In light of His teaching, what are some ways we can be faithful servants and occupy till He comes?

What are some ways that Satan works in the church or in the lives of believers to distract them from carrying out this command?

Targeted Truth 6: Believers will be raptured before the tribulation.

There are some who say that the word *rapture* doesn't appear in the Bible, but they're incorrect. Where do we get the word *rapture* from? (See page 25 in *Has the Tribulation Begun?*)

What promise do the following verses make to believers about the coming time of wrath, or the tribulation?

1 Thessalonians 1:10—

1 Thessalonians 5:9—

Revelation 3:10—

Why do you think a denial of the rapture will naturally have a negative impact on the church?

DEEP-SEATED DECEPTION

What do the following verses say about the way Satan carries out his works of deception?

Genesis 3:1, 13—

2 Corinthians 4:4—

2 Corinthians 11:14—

What instructions are we given about protecting ourselves?

2 Corinthians 10:4-5—

James 4:7—

1 Peter 5:8-9—

"Truth is under assault. Satan has already garnered a tremendous victory in the world through his lies. Sadly, he also has a foothold in the church, which continues to strengthen. Will his deceptions ever end? Thankfully, they will…There will come a time when the devil will be shut up so that he can't deceive anymore."

Has the Tribulation Begun?, pages 26-27

TURNING OUR KNOWLEDGE INTO ACTION

In this lesson, we've seen how an ignorance of what the Bible says about the end times can hurt the church and individual believers. In the space below, write a list of the benefits we can gain from being well informed about God's plans for the future. Think of as many as you can.

2

THE TROUBLE
WITH JACOB

Everything God does has a purpose. Every person and event plays a role in God's master plan for the ages.

In Isaiah 46:9-10, we read,

> Remember the former things of old,
> for I am God, and there is no other;
> I am God, and there is none like Me,
> declaring the end from the beginning,
> and from ancient times things that are not yet done,
> saying, "My counsel shall stand,
> and I will do all My pleasure."

Those words make it clear that God is totally sovereign. What He decides to do, He will do. He alone is God, and no one can withstand His will.

Even the things that are evil have their purpose. Consider what Peter said in Acts 2:23 about Jesus' crucifixion: "Him, being delivered by the determined purpose and foreknowl-edge of God, you have taken by lawless hands, have cruci-fied, and put to death."

Though at the crucifixion Satan and people conspired to do evil against Jesus, they were actually carrying out God's "determined purpose."

Again, everything God does has a reason. And that includes the tribulation. Through the judgments that take place, He will accomplish, among other things, His desired work in the people of Israel.

> "Jacob is Israel. Jacob's trouble is Israel's trouble. It is for Israel that the tribulation has been designed. Yes, there will be wrath upon the unbelieving world for their rejection of God and His free gift of salvation. But Jeremiah does not call this terrible time 'global trouble' or 'world trouble,' or even 'unbelievers' trouble.' This period is directed toward Jacob with the purpose of bringing the Jewish people to the point that they are ready to accept the Messiah they have rejected. It is then at the end of the trouble that, as Paul wrote, 'All Israel will be saved' (Romans 11:26)."
>
> *Has the Tribulation Begun?*, page 31

Speaking of the tribulation, the prophet Jeremiah said,

Alas! For that day is great,
so that none is like it,
and it is the time of Jacob's trouble,
but he shall be saved out of it (Jeremiah 30:7).

The seven-year tribulation is called "the time of Jacob's trouble," and is given other names as well. In the following passages, what terms are used to describe this time of wrath?

Isaiah 34:8—

Zephaniah 1:15—

Joel 2:2—

Revelation 6:16-17—

GOD AND ISRAEL

Read Genesis 12:1-3. In this passage, what three or four specific promises does God make to Abram?

Note the words "you shall be a blessing" and "in you all the families of the earth will be blessed." What was God's intention for the nation of Israel? (See page 32.)

On page 33 of *Has the Tribulation Begun?*, we read, "So often it takes affliction to bring us to God." Why do you think this is so?

According to Genesis 17:17, why did Abraham doubt he would have an heir that would begin the fulfillment of God's promise to make him a great nation?

What does the fact that Abraham and Sarah were able to conceive Isaac say about God? What do you think God wanted to proclaim to the world by doing this?

After the Roman destruction of Jerusalem and the temple in AD 70, the people of Israel were scattered worldwide. What promise did God make to His people in Ezekiel 36:23-24?

And to whom did the land belong, according to God Himself?

Read Zechariah 13:8-9. What did God say would happen to the people of Israel during—and at the end—of the tribulation?

"As Paul wrote, a 'blindness in part has happened to Israel' (Romans 11:25). The tribulation will prepare their eyes to be opened, so that when Jesus returns, they will look at Him whom they have pierced and they will mourn as a sign of their repentance. It is this repentance that leads to a forgiveness that brings salvation."

Has the Tribulation Begun?, page 37

THE ENEMY AND ISRAEL

On page 37 of *Has the Tribulation Begun?*, we read that "whatever God loves the devil hates. Nowhere is this more evident than in Satan's passionate hatred for the Jews, God's chosen people." For what reasons do you think Satan would want to destroy Israel?

If Satan had been able to keep Christ from being born, what would the consequences have been?

THE WORLD AND ISRAEL

On page 40 of *Has the Tribulation Begun?*, we read, "People are fascinated with that which is different."

Read Leviticus 20:26. What was the primary way God wanted His chosen people to be different?

What are some other ways they were to differ, according to Leviticus 19:3-4, 37?

What are some Jewish customs people today are curious about or fascinated by?

On page 43 of *Has the Tribulation Begun?*, we read, "Satan hates the Jews. Therefore, he will do all he can to sustain antisemitism throughout the world." Why would it make sense that, as we approach the end times, antisemitism will get worse?

THE CHURCH AND ISRAEL

There are some who say Israel is no longer part of God's plan for today or the future. They say that the church has replaced Israel.

But in Genesis 12:1-3, when God made His promise to Israel, notice His repetitious use of the phrase, "I will." And in Genesis 15, when God set up His covenant with Abraham, God alone walked between the animal pieces while Abraham slept. This meant God alone was obligated to fulfill the covenant.

According to Genesis 17:7-8, how long was God's covenant with Abraham and his descendants (Israel) to last?

What incredible promise did God make to His people in Leviticus 26:44?

How long did God promise to preserve His people, according to Psalm 121:8?

"Since Abraham was first called out of Ur, the people of Israel have belonged to God. He loved them, and He loves them still. He wanted a relationship with them, and He wants it still. This is the foundational purpose for the tribulation. God loves the people of Israel, and He wants them back. But He wants them to *want* to come back. At the end of the seven years of the tribulation, they will do just that."

Has the Tribulation Begun?, pages 47-48

TURNING OUR KNOWLEDGE INTO ACTION

Scripture makes it clear that God's promises to Israel are forever promises. He has not cast aside His chosen people; He is still working through them today and will continue to do so during the tribulation.

In the same way that God is committed to keeping His promises to Israel, He will keep His promises to you. What does that tell you about God's love for you?

And what is an appropriate response to God for His faithfulness to us?

3

A QUESTION
OF OVERKILL

As people read the book of Revelation, a stark truth stands out about the tribulation: This will be a serious time of judgment. As the seven years go by, God's wrath will increase in intensity. Never in earth's history have horrific events occurred on this scale—all past tragedies will be minor in comparison.

And people wonder: Will God be too severe?

Yet as early as Genesis 3:15, in the Garden of Eden, we see that God is a God of mercy. After Adam and Eve fell into sin, God immediately promised that one day, a Savior would come to rescue them. All through the pages of the Bible, the Lord's mercy is evident in His care for His people, in the miracles He did on their behalf, and in keeping His promises.

We also see that whenever God poured out judgments, He consistently gave warnings. Second Peter 2:5 says Noah was "a preacher of righteousness." At the time God commanded

Noah to build the ark, He said man's "days shall be one hundred and twenty years" (Genesis 6:3). We also know from 1 Peter 3:20 that "the Divine longsuffering waited in the days of Noah, while the ark was being prepared." Similar warnings were given to Israel and other nations all through biblical history.

Yes, God "is longsuffering toward us, not willing that any should perish but that all should come to repentance" (2 Peter 3:9). When it comes to judgment, the Lord is patient. But eventually there comes a point when judgment must come.

The penalty for sin is the same for all. "There is none righteous, no, not one," says Romans 3:10. "All have sinned and fall short of the glory of God" (Romans 3:23). And "the wages of sin is death, but the gift of God is eternal life in Christ Jesus our Lord" (Romans 6:23).

So God does provide a way out—eternal life in Christ Jesus. That's His mercy. But those who reject His mercy will face His judgment.

The tribulation, severe as it is, has its purposes. God will use that time to do His work. Though we may not fully understand why unrepentant hearts are deserving of such punishment, we can rest in the truths that God is patient and merciful, and that He does not want any to perish.

"The tribulation is primarily about disciplining the Jews so that they will finally be brought to the point that they will look upon the One whom they have pierced and respond with mourning and repentance. However, there is also a punitive nature to the seven years of horror. The wider purpose of the tribulation includes bringing wrath upon the world as a just recompense for the sins of mankind."

Has the Tribulation Begun?, page 51

On page 52 of *Has the Tribulation Begun?*, we read, "To understand the tribulation, we must understand sin." How do you think God views sin?

Why do you think sin grieves God so greatly?

SIN'S TRAGIC EFFECTS

The Moral State of the World

Isaiah 5:20 says, "Woe to those who call evil good, and good evil." In today's world, what are some examples of evil being called good?

What about some examples of good being called evil?

In John 3:19, we read that "men loved darkness rather than light." What does this tell you about the inclinations of fallen mankind?

Read Jeremiah 17:9. How does this passage describe the human heart?

According to what we read on pages 54-55 of *Has the Tribulation Begun?*, what are the three moral indicators that lead to the decline of an empire?

1.

2.

3.

The Geopolitical State of the World

Considering what we have learned about sin so far—that all have sinned, and that the heart is deceitful—why do you think the kingdoms of this world are always destined to fail?

Why do you think Satan takes pleasure in battles that take place between people and nations?

The Physical State of the World

Romans 8:20-22 says that because of mankind's sin, "the creation was subjected to futility, not willingly…we know that the whole creation groans and labors with birth pangs together until now." What does this tell you about the effects of sin on this world?

What promise does Romans 8:21 make about what will happen when Christ returns and we receive our glorified bodies?

The Spiritual State of the World

Read Ephesians 2:1-3. Before receiving Christ, what were we dead in?

What did we walk according to?

How did we conduct ourselves?

Next, read Ephesians 2:12. What do those who are without Christ lack?

Based on these descriptions in Ephesians 2:2-3, 12, how serious would you say sin is?

WHAT IS SIN?

What concise definition of sin is given on page 62 of *Has the Tribulation Begun?*

What are some ways that you see people rebelling against God today?

When people reject God, what are they saying…

about who should rule on the throne of their heart?

about His wisdom regarding what is right and what is wrong?

According to Romans 2:15, how can we say, with certainty, that even unbelievers know when they are doing something wrong?

In light of what we've learned about sin, why can we say the tribulation won't be too severe?

The most amazing thing of all about God's mercy is that He does not expect us to try to save ourselves from our sin. It's impossible for us to do so. He took upon Himself the task of making salvation possible for us. What simple way can we be freed from our sin, according to Romans 10:9-10?

"If you are afraid of the coming tribulation, let the Messiah remove that fear. Repent of your sins, turn to Jesus, and receive Him into your life. Let today be the day of your salvation!"

Has the Tribulation Begun?, page 64

TURNING OUR KNOWLEDGE INTO ACTION

As you look back on this lesson, what have you learned about the seriousness of sin?

What influence should this have on your pursuit of personal holiness?

What have you learned about the greatness of God's mercy?

Spend some time in prayer now, thanking God for the gift of salvation and His great mercy.

4

ORDER AND MERCY

We cannot escape our sin. We're in bondage to it. As Ephesians 2:1 says, before receiving Christ as Savior, we are "dead in trespasses and sins." Those who are spiritually dead cannot come to spiritual life on their own. They are entirely incapable of doing anything that can lead to their salvation.

In fact, before salvation in Christ, the apostle Paul describes us as "slaves of sin" (Romans 6:20). Our only hope of escaping sin's bondage had to come from outside of us—from God Himself. So great is God's mercy that He reached down to us even when we were His enemies. As Romans 5:8 proclaims, "God demonstrates His own love toward us, in that while we were still sinners, Christ died for us."

This demonstrates the greatness of God's love for us—that He would make redemption possible when we rejected Him and had absolutely nothing to offer Him.

What more could we ask for?

"All have sinned. Therefore, all humanity is deserving of punishment, and the ultimate punishment is eternal separation from God. That is the spiritual death that Paul said we each earn through our sins—our 'wages.' Jews deserve it because of their rebellious choices and their rejection of the Messiah. Gentiles deserve spiritual death for the very same reasons. Each person who has ever been born has bought the car, and now we are facing a debt that we can't pay. The penalty for our actions is just."

Has the Tribulation Begun?, page 65

GOD OF ORDER

All around us, we see visible signs of God's orderliness. What are some examples of His order that you appreciate?

Order in Salvation—Two Births

Read John 3:16. What means did God provide for us to be freed from sin and be able to enjoy a relationship with Him?

When Nicodemus asked, "How can a man be born when he is old? Can he enter a second time into his mother's womb and be born?" (John 3:4), how did Jesus respond? (See vv. 5-6.)

The term *born again* describes the second birth. What does it mean to be born again?

What does 2 Corinthians 5:17 say about those who are born again, who are "in Christ"?

Order in Consequences—Two Deaths

Just as there are two births, a physical birth and a spiritual birth, there are also two deaths, also physical and spiritual.

In *Has the Tribulation Begun?*, we read, "Up until the resurrection of Jesus, everyone went down to Sheol" (page 71). According to Luke 16:22-23, what are the two areas of Sheol?

Who inhabits those two areas?

Read 2 Corinthians 5:6-8. At the resurrection, what change did Jesus make for the location of the believing dead?

Why should Christians have no fear of physical death?

What truth does Revelation 20:6 proclaim to believers about the second death (physical death)?

Read Hebrews 9:27. Why is physical death so terrible for unbelievers?

Order in Restoration—Two Resurrections

At death, the eternal soul is separated from its temporal body. According to 1 Corinthians 15:42, what will eventually happen to the bodies of both unbelievers and believers?

Read Revelation 20:6. Which resurrection will believers take part in?

What will those who have part in the first resurrection do?

What transformation does 1 Corinthians 15:51-55 say will occur to the bodies of believers at the first resurrection?

According to John 5:28-29, who will be raised up in the second resurrection, or the "resurrection of condemnation"?

Read Revelation 20:11-16. What will be God's sole purpose for raising up those who take part in the second resurrection?

Order in Justice—Seven Future Judgments

On pages 80-85 of *Has the Tribulation Begun?* are listed seven different judgments. Write them here:

1.

2.

3.

4.

5.

6.

7.

According to 1 Corinthians 3:12-15, what will happen at the bema seat judgment?

While we as believers still have time here on earth, how can we best prepare for the bema seat judgment?

A TRIBULATION OF MERCY

On page 86 in *Has the Tribulation Begun?*, we read, "In times of suffering, people will typically react one of two ways." What are those two ways?

In what way does 2 Peter 3:8-9 confirm the great extent of God's mercy?

"The Lord could have bypassed the tribulation. He could have just said, 'I'm tired of you rebels, be you Jew or Gentile. You're destined for hell, so you might as well go now.' Instead, He will give one last seven-year reprieve, telling all humanity, 'Now is the day of your salvation. Come to Me today. Because very soon it will be too late.'"

Has the Tribulation Begun?, page 87

TURNING OUR KNOWLEDGE INTO ACTION

Believers should have no fear of appearing before Christ's judgment seat, for this is not a judgment about salvation, but about our works. Carefully read 1 Corinthians 3:12-15. What kinds of works do you think would fit in the category of wood, hay, and straw?

What kinds of works do you think would fit in the category of gold, silver, and precious stones?

As you consider your thoughts, words, and actions, where do you see room for growth in the kinds of works you are producing as a believer?

5

THE DAY OF
DEPARTURE

The rapture is one topic many believers have questions about. Scripture reveals just enough information that we know it is an event we can look forward to. Yet there are still some aspects of the rapture that are shrouded in mystery—especially its timing.

Jesus makes the first New Testament mention of the rapture. When He spoke about the many mansions in His Father's house, He said, "I go to prepare a place for you. And if I go and prepare a place for you, I will come again and receive you to Myself; that where I am, there you may be also" (John 14:2-3). And later, Paul wrote that when the rapture happens, we will "meet the Lord in the air. And thus we shall always be with the Lord" (1 Thessalonians 4:17).

It is no wonder, then, that the Bible describes the rapture as "the blessed hope"! (Titus 2:13). The truth that we will one day be reunited with our Lord and be with Him forever should excite us. In the same way that we look forward to taking a trip to a destination we've never visited, we should have great anticipation for this event that assures us we will go to heaven before the tribulation begins.

> "The tribulation is coming. But not only did God provide the means for us to escape it, but He clearly spelled out His plan so that we wouldn't be afraid. That plan is the rapture. The rapture is a wonderful gift from our loving and merciful God that should give us hope and peace. It should also motivate us to let others know how they, too, can escape the coming wrath, and join us in living today without fear of the future."
>
> *Has the Tribulation Begun?*, page 90

A BIBLICAL RAPTURE

What does the Greek New Testament word *harpazo* mean?

How many times is it used, and what do five of those instances refer to?

In 1 Thessalonians 4:16-17, Paul wrote,

> The Lord Himself will descend from heaven with a shout, with the voice of an archangel, and with the trumpet of God. And the dead in Christ will rise first. Then we who are alive and remain shall be caught up together with them in the clouds to meet the Lord in the air. And thus we shall always be with the Lord.

What will physically happen to believers when the rapture occurs?

Read the following passages, and write what happened physically to those involved:

Genesis 5:24—

2 Kings 2:11—

Luke 24:51—

Why a Rapture?—Saved from Wrath

During the tribulation, God will pour out His wrath upon all who live on the earth. Biblically speaking, why does it *not* make sense for believers to go through the tribulation?

John 5:24—

Romans 5:9—

Romans 8:1—

Romans 8:33-34—

What do the following passages say about Christians and God's wrath?

1 Thessalonians 1:10—

1 Thessalonians 5:9-10—

Revelation 3:10—

Why a Rapture?—To Be with Jesus

Shortly before His crucifixion, Jesus told His disciples He would soon leave them (John 13:33). When they became distressed over this news, what encouragement did Jesus offer in John 14:1?

And immediately after offering that encouragement, what promise did Jesus give in verses 2-3?

When Paul wrote about this same event—the rapture—in 1 Thessalonians 4:13-18, what did he say our forever destination would be? (See verse 17.)

Why a Rapture?—To Carry Out the Bema Seat Judgment

After the rapture, where will we be taken, according to 2 Corinthians 5:9-10?

What will be the purpose of this event?

Why can we say with certainty that the bema seat judgment has nothing to do with our salvation?

What clue in Revelation 19:8 do we see that reveals all believers will appear before the judgment seat of Christ between the rapture (being taken up to heaven) and the second coming (returning to earth with the Savior)?

Why a Rapture?—To Ring the Wedding Bells

We know from Revelation 19:6-9 that the church, who is the bride, will be married to Christ, the Groom, in heaven.

Read Ephesians 5:25-27. Here, Scripture compares the marriage of Christ and the church to a marriage between a husband and wife. According to verse 26, what is Christ doing today, before we are raptured, to prepare us?

What does verse 26 say about how this washing is done?

For what purpose does Christ do this cleansing, according to verse 27?

What is the appropriate response to what Christ has done on our behalf? (See Isaiah 61:10.)

WHO IS THE RAPTURE FOR?

Based on what we learned earlier from 1 Thessalonians 1:10, 1 Thessalonians 5:9-10, and Revelation 3:10, who is the rapture for?

"The rapture belongs to the church. It is our Savior's way of removing us from a terrible situation in which we don't belong and taking us to where we do belong. In fact, the place to which He is taking us is one that He has specially prepared for us for that exact time. So, if you are a believer in Jesus Christ, be excited!"

Has the Tribulation Begun?, page 107

TURNING OUR KNOWLEDGE INTO ACTION

In Titus 2:13, the apostle Paul describes the rapture as "the blessed hope." Why should all believers look forward to the rapture?

In what ways do you personally see it as a blessing and a source of hope?

Why do you think it is so important for believers to live with an eternal perspective that looks forward to the future?

6

A MATTER
OF TIMING

When it comes to the rapture, there are different views about the timing. Will it occur before, during, throughout, or after the tribulation?

Some are very vigorous about defending their view. Others say it's not really possible to know, and that the timing of the rapture is not all that important.

But if the subject of the rapture appears in Scripture, and we are called to rightly divide the "word of truth" (2 Timothy 2:15), then we ought to at least make an earnest attempt to have as clear an understanding of the rapture as possible.

In the New Testament epistles, we find numerous mentions of the rapture. In fact, when the apostle Paul wrote to the believers in Thessalonica, one reason he did so was to clear up some confusion people had about the event. There were some unscrupulous teachers spreading falsehoods about the rapture and tribulation, and Paul wanted to make sure the Thessalonian church had correct information.

All of this speaks to the importance of this event and our understanding of it. With that in mind, let's take some time to carefully examine what God's Word says.

> "The timing of the rapture is very important. It tells us much about who God is and how He treats those who follow Him. It also is a determining factor in how we will spend the time we have left on this earth. If the rapture could happen at any moment, then we should have a sense of urgency about how we spend our time."
>
> *Has the Tribulation Begun?*, page 110

Let's look now at the five major views for the timing of the rapture.

PARTIAL RAPTURE

Those who advocate this view teach that believers will be raptured at different points during the tribulation, depending on how much punishment is required to purify them.

Based on what we read on pages 111-112 of *Has the Tribulation Begun?*, what three reasons can we give for disqualifying this view?

1.

2.

3.

MID-TRIB RAPTURE

Some say that only the last half of the tribulation will be all that bad, and that the first half will be relatively quiet.

But what major events do we see happen right at the beginning of the tribulation, according to Revelation chapter 6, when Jesus first breaks open the seven-sealed scroll?

What should the lack of any Scripture passages about a rapture of Christians occurring *during* the tribulation tell us?

To arrive at the mid-trib rapture view requires eisegesis rather than exegesis. What is the difference between the two? (See page 113 of *Has the Tribulation Begun?*)

PRE-WRATH RAPTURE

How do those who hold to the pre-wrath rapture view use Revelation 13:7, Revelation 17:6, and Matthew 24:22 in their attempt to prove the church will still be on earth during at least part of the tribulation?

Is every saint or elect person necessarily a member of the church? Explain. (See pages 114-115 in *Has the Tribulation Begun?*)

What problem arises when one attempts to separate the seven years of God's judgment into three sections, as done by advocates of the pre-wrath rapture (the beginning of sorrows, the great tribulation, the day of the Lord)?

POST-TRIB RAPTURE

This view says the rapture will happen at the end of the tribulation.

What do those who hold to the post-trib rapture view say about the events described in Matthew 24 and the book of Revelation?

Why is this incompatible with a literal interpretation of the Bible? (See page 116 in *Has the Tribulation Begun?*)

On page 116 of *Has the Tribulation Begun?*, we read, "Once the allegorical approach to interpreting Scripture becomes a viable option, then it becomes very easy to make the Bible say anything you want it to say." Why do you think interpreting the Bible allegorically can be dangerous?

What are the two logical problems with the post-trib rapture view? (See pages 116-117 in *Has the Tribulation Begun?*)

1.

2.

PRE-TRIB RAPTURE

How do we know that the pre-trib rapture view is not a recent development—what did the following early church writers say?

Ephraem the Syrian—

Irenaeus—

Some who argue against the pre-trib view say that the church deserves some suffering. But as we already learned earlier, how do the following verses dispute that argument?

Romans 5:9—

Romans 8:1—

1 Thessalonians 1:10—

1 Thessalonians 5:9-10—

Pre-Trib Argument 1: God's Pattern Is to Remove the Righteous Before Wrath

Whom did God remove before He poured out His wrath through the flood? (See Genesis 7:1-4.)

Whom did God spare before He judged Sodom and Gomorrah? (See Genesis 19:15-17.)

What pattern does this set for Christ's bride, the church, with regard to the tribulation?

Pre-Trib Argument 2: Christ's Return Is Imminent

In Revelation 22:7, 12, Jesus said, "I am coming quickly." What did Jesus mean when He said this? (See page 121 in *Has the Tribulation Begun?*)

How is the truth that Christ's coming could have been imminent in Paul's day affirmed in Paul's words in 1 Thessalonians 4:15-18?

Pre-Trib Argument 3: The Son's Work Is Sufficient for the Father

What is the significance of Jesus' words "It is finished!" in John 19:30?

Is there any further penalty that needs to be paid for our justification? What one or two Scripture passages can you think of that confirm that?

Pre-Trib Argument 4: A Literal Interpretation of Scripture

Is the church mentioned anywhere in Revelation chapters 4–18?

Some say that the absence of the church in Revelation 4–18 is an argument from silence. Why does that reasoning fall apart in light of Revelation 1–3?

Read 1 Corinthians 15:51-56 and 1 Thessalonians 4:13-18. Both speak about the rapture. Is there any hint at all in these passages that the rapture will take place during the tribulation itself?

Pre-Trib Argument 5: The Twofold Purpose of the Tribulation

Jeremiah 30:7 describes the tribulation as "the time of Jacob's trouble." Jacob is the Old Testament patriarch who fathered the sons who began the 12 tribes of Israel. With that in mind, would it be more correct to say God's purpose for the tribulation is to discipline Israel, or the church?

If the church has already been made pure by Christ, what purpose is there for the church to go through the tribulation?

Pre-Trib Argument 6: A True Comfort

When Paul taught the believers in Thessaloniki about the rapture, what did he say they were to do with this knowledge, according to 1 Thessalonians 4:18?

"My friend, we are not appointed to wrath. As the church, there 'is therefore now no condemnation to those who are in Christ Jesus, who do not walk according to the flesh, but according to the Spirit' (Romans 8:1). Yes, we will have tribulations—some more than others. But for those who are in Christ Jesus, we will not have *the* tribulation. Jesus is coming to remove the church, His bride, before the judgment begins."

Has the Tribulation Begun?, page 125

TURNING OUR KNOWLEDGE INTO ACTION

In this lesson, we've looked at six strong arguments in support of the pre-trib rapture view. In what ways have you been encouraged or edified by these?

What one or two arguments did you appreciate most, and why?

7

SAVE THE DATE

One of the most intriguing questions about the rapture is, When will it happen? Many people through the ages have speculated about this and set dates. Every single human prediction has failed.

For anyone to even try to guess the date is foolish in light of what Jesus said: "Of that day and hour no one knows, not even the angels of heaven, but My Father only" (Matthew 24:36). This stands as an admonishment against any attempts to figure out the timing of the rapture.

What's remarkable is that the Bible is filled with information about the end times—in both the Old and New Testaments. There are hundreds of prophecies in Scripture relating to the tribulation and the second coming of Christ. And yet God chose to not reveal the timing of the rapture. Clearly this was intentional on His part.

However, that doesn't mean we're left completely in the dark. Shortly before Jesus was crucified, He spoke at length to His disciples about the signs that would indicate when the end times are drawing near. The information He provided can be used to determine the general season in which we can expect the rapture and the onset of the tribulation to occur.

> "We'll never pinpoint the precise moment of Jesus' return for His church. But the Bible does give us tools so that we can determine the likely time frame."
>
> *Has the Tribulation Begun?*, page 129

Why do you think the Father has intentionally been secretive about the specific timing of Christ's return?

WHEN IS THE SEASON?

Timing Tool 1: Bible Prophecy

On pages 129-130 of *Has the Tribulation Begun?*, we read, "God filled nearly a third of the Bible with talk of future events." Why is this so?

What are we told about the origin of prophecy in 2 Peter 1:20-21?

To make sure we don't force our own perspectives into Scripture, we must interpret it literally and ask, "What was the author's original intent?" Why do you think it's so important to ask this question when we attempt to understand the Bible?

Why do you think a careful look at the context of a passage is crucial as well?

In addition, why is it vital for us to compare different prophecy passages to one another?

Timing Tool 2: Current Events

In Matthew 24:4-8, what types of events did Christ say would serve as indicators that we are approaching the tribulation?

In verse 8, Jesus described these signs as "the beginning of sorrows," which can also be understood to mean "birth pangs." What do you see taking place today that could line up with what Jesus described in Matthew 24:4-8?

Timing Tool 3: God and Israel

In Deuteronomy 30:3-5, what did God promise He would do to the nation of Israel after it had been scattered to all the nations?

Some say the prophecy in Deuteronomy 30:3-5 was fulfilled when the Jews returned to Israel after the Babylonian exile. But why does it make more sense for the rebirth of Israel in 1948 to be the fulfillment?

Israel declared its independence on May 14, 1948. What prophecy in Isaiah 66:8 was fulfilled when this occurred?

"How close is the tribulation? An Israeli state is necessary for the events of the tribulation to occur. For 2,000 years, there was no Israeli state. Now, there is not only an Israeli state, but it is thriving."

Has the Tribulation Begun?, page 135

Timing Tool 4: Ezekiel 36–39

Ezekiel 36, which was written more than 2,000 years ago, promised that one day Israel would become a revitalized land, which has happened. Ezekiel 37 speaks of a revitalized people, and there are many Jews in the land today.

Then Ezekiel 38, which is still future, tells us what will happen "in the latter days" (v. 16). We're told about an invasion that will come against Israel.

Where will this attack come from, according to verse 6?

How do verses 9 and 16 describe the size of this invading force?

This prophecy serves as confirmation that it is necessary for the nation of Israel to be in place so that it's possible for the tribulation to occur.

Timing Tool 5: The Parable of the Fig Tree

What will the budding of the fig tree indicate, as taught in Jesus' parable in Matthew 24:32-35?

In the parable, why does it make sense for the fig tree to represent Israel?

According to what we read on page 141 of *Has the Tribulation Begun?*, what generation was Jesus referring to in Matthew 24:34?

WHEN IS THE DATE?

Even with all the clues that help us to know the season of Christ's return, why is it still best to avoid getting caught up in the date trap?

"What does *soon* mean? It could mean hours, days, months, or years. What I can encourage you with is that we are the first people in the history of the church who can truly say that it will not happen generations from now. Never before has soon been so soon. So, be encouraged. While we can't know the exact date, it is undoubtedly around the corner."

Has the Tribulation Begun?, page 142

TURNING OUR KNOWLEDGE INTO ACTION

The whole matter of not knowing the exact time of the rapture brings up an important point: Even when God chooses *not* to reveal something, we are still to trust in His perfect wisdom about what He will do, and when. What are some examples, from your personal experience, of circumstances in which you didn't know what to expect, and you had to place greater trust in God?

In what ways can we benefit from trusting God when it comes to things we don't know or understand?

8

EVERYWHERE A SIGN

Though we should never attempt to set a specific date for Christ's return, Jesus clearly wanted us to know the season. That's why we should pay close attention to what He said about the signs that will precede His coming. He didn't reveal this information merely to inform us, but to shape how we live.

> "As we look through the signs of the end times, both the birth pangs and the global preparations, we will see just how close we are to our time running out on this earth. My prayer is that one of two actions will take place in your heart as a result. If you are not a Christian, I hope that you will be motivated to give your life to Christ now while there is still time…If you are a Christian, I trust that when you see how the stage is set for the Lord's return, that your love for those around you will kick into high gear, moving you to share the

truth with them so that they, too, can be rescued from the tribulation that is soon to come."

Has the Tribulation Begun?, page 144

THE SIGNS OF THE TIMES

Sign 1: Wars and Rumors of War

What are some examples of places where hostilities are occurring around the world right now?

Based on Ezekiel 38:2-6, which countries are among those that will join forces in the unholy alliance that will come against Israel?

Why will this military coalition attack Israel, according to Ezekiel 38:10-13?

Sign 2: Famines

In Matthew 24:7, what did Jesus say would be among the signs indicating the nearness of His coming?

According to what we read on page 149 of *Has the Tribulation Begun?*, what nations are currently facing critical food shortages?

How do you think wars and energy crises can make famines worse?

Sign 3: Pestilences

When the COVID-19 pandemic broke out in early 2020, the world got a taste of the kind of panic pestilence can create. What were some of the major effects the COVID pandemic had on people and countries?

Why is it likely that governments and world leaders would be in favor of another global health crisis? (See page 149 of *Has the Tribulation Begun?*)

Sign 4: Earthquakes

In what two ways are earthquakes increasing?

What natural disaster is not mentioned in the Olivet Discourse, and what are some places that have been affected by it? (See page 150 in *Has the Tribulation Begun?*)

Sign 5: Globalism

Global Government

When the antichrist ascends to power, what will the people of different nations be willing to do?

What do the member nations of the European Union share, and what is this helping to prepare for? (See page 153 in *Has the Tribulation Begun?*)

How are people likely to respond after millions suddenly disappear in the rapture?

What might people be willing to give up their freedoms in exchange for?

Global Economy

What two or three examples do you personally see of how closely interconnected countries are through their economies?

Global Culture

What is the main reason that the world is smaller than it has ever been?

What are television, movies, and social media seeking to present as acceptable?

What impact is technology having on moral standards?

Global Religion

On pages 156-157 of *Has the Tribulation Begun?*, we read that the antichrist "will not just be a political leader, but a spiritual one. Not only will he unite people's minds, but he will draw in their hearts, their loyalty, and their adoration." Why do you think this combination of being both a political and spiritual leader will make the antichrist so dangerous?

How do you think a global zeal for environmentalism can be used by powerful leaders to unify people?

THE STAGE IS SET

As you look around you, what are some ways you see our world shifting more and more to a global mindset?

In what ways do you think a world that is driven by a global mindset would make conditions ripe for the rise of the antichrist?

"Can I give you a date for the rapture or for when the tribulation will begin? I'm sorry, I can't. No one can. I can reassure you, though, that we are not only in the last generation, but we are in the time within the last generation in which everything is in place for the curtain to rise at any moment."

Has the Tribulation Begun?, page 158

TURNING OUR KNOWLEDGE INTO ACTION

Based on what Jesus taught in Matthew 24, it is clear that we are rapidly approaching the end times. To what extent is the awareness of this reality having an impact on how you live?

What changes are you compelled to make to your personal life or your priorities in the light of the nearness of Christ's coming?

9

THE EMPEROR AND THE POLITICIAN

Up to now, we've looked at some of the evidence that tells us the tribulation has not started yet. One big reason is because the church is still present on the earth. We know from Scripture passages like 1 Thessalonians 1:10 and 5:9-10 that the church is not destined for God's wrath. Instead, it will be removed from the earth in the rapture, and all church-age believers will be taken up to meet the Lord in the air.

But we know that time is running out. In the last lesson, we looked at some signs that serve as evidence we're rapidly approaching the end times. At some point in the future, the rapture *will* happen. And though God does not tell us about the specific date it will occur, He gives clues about the season. And significantly, He tells us a lot about what will occur during the tribulation.

Once again, God has not provided prophecies merely to inform us. Prophecy is meant to stir us to action, as we'll see in this lesson. And this call to action is for both believers and unbelievers.

"We've spent a lot of time looking at why we are not currently in the tribulation. But for those of you reading this book who may not have taken that step of receiving Jesus as your Savior and Lord, I thought it might be helpful to let you know how you can be sure that the tribulation actually has begun."

Has the Tribulation Begun?, pages 159-160

SEVEN FULL YEARS OF WRATH

Read 2 Thessalonians 2:6-8 carefully:

Now you know what is restraining, that he may be revealed in his own time. For the mystery of lawlessness is already at work; only He who now restrains will do so until He is taken out of the way. And then the lawless one will be revealed, whom the Lord will consume with the breath of His mouth and destroy with the brightness of His coming.

"He who now restrains" refers to the Holy Spirit and His presence and work in born-again believers. In the tribulation, the Holy Spirit will continue to work on earth as He did in the Old Testament. But His work in and through the church will no longer be part of this world. What will be revealed when this occurs?

Because the Spirit is present in every believer, the Spirit's influence on this world is great. It's holding back the tide of sin. But once the church is gone, that restraining influence will also be gone. In what ways do you think our world will decline after the church is removed from the earth?

What does John 10:10 tell us about Satan?

Read Revelation 13:2. What will the dragon (Satan) grant to the beast (the antichrist)?

What does this tell you about what the antichrist will be like?

In Daniel 8:1-12, we read of a vision the prophet Daniel had. What did the angel Gabriel say this vision referred to, according to verse 17?

What additional information did Gabriel give in verse 19?

Read Daniel 8:11, Matthew 24:15, and 2 Thessalonians 2:4. All three passages speak of an act the antichrist will carry out at the midpoint of the tribulation—he will desecrate the temple. What does 2 Thessalonians 2:4 specifically say the antichrist will do when he carries out this act?

A key observation: In Daniel 8, the Hebrew word *zaam*, which is translated "wrath, rage, indignation," speaks of what will happen during the entirety of the tribulation. In the Greek translation of the Old Testament book of Daniel, the apostle Paul uses *orge*. Paul used this word in reference to the entire tribulation, which is why we know God's wrath will be poured out all seven years, and not just during the second half.

DUAL FULFILLMENT

Some prophecies in the Bible have dual fulfillments. For example, in Isaiah 7:13-17, we see both a near fulfillment and a future one:

Hear now, O house of David! Is it a small thing for you to weary men, but will you weary my God also? Therefore the Lord Himself will give you a sign: Behold, the virgin shall conceive and bear a Son, and shall call His name Immanuel. Curds and honey He shall eat, that He may know to refuse the evil and choose the good. For before the Child shall know to refuse the evil and choose the good, the land that you dread will be forsaken by both her kings. The Lord will bring the king of Assyria upon you and your people and your father's house—days that have not come since the day that Ephraim departed from Judah.

What is the near fulfillment of this passage? (See page 165 in *Has the Tribulation Begun?*)

What is the distant fulfillment?

Now let's turn to the near and future fulfillments in Daniel 8. As you answer the upcoming questions, carefully follow the overview provided on pages 166-173 of *Has the Tribulation Begun?*

The Near Fulfillment

What does the powerful animal in Daniel 8:3-4 represent?

Which empire did this animal overthrow?

Which conqueror and empire does the goat in Daniel 8:5-7 represent?

What does this goat do to the ram?

When the conquering goat arrived in Jerusalem and walked to the Temple Mount, why did he end up ordering that the temple not be destroyed?

When the single horn on the goat was broken, it was replaced by four new horns (Daniel 8:8-9). Who did these horns represent?

In relation to the prophecy in Daniel 8, only one of the four horns is significant. The Seleucid horn was eventually led by Antiochus III the Great, who set the stage for the little horn who came next, Antiochus IV. How does Daniel 8:25 describe Antiochus IV?

Antiochus IV designated himself as Epiphanes. What does *Epiphanes* mean?

When Antiochus IV made this proclamation, what did he expect people to do in response?

What ethnic group refused to worship Antiochus IV, and why?

What did Antiochus IV do in response to the Jews?

What did the Jewish uprising under Judas Maccabeus accomplish, and what famous Jewish holiday did this give birth to?

All of this shows the near fulfillment of the prophecies in Daniel 8. Now let's look at the future, greater fulfillment.

The Future Fulfillment

How will Antiochus IV and the antichrist compare?

Just as Antiochus IV declared himself to be God, what will the antichrist do, according to Daniel 7:25 and 2 Thessalonians 2:4?

What warning did Jesus give to the Jews in Matthew 24:15-16 that indicates just how wicked the antichrist will be?

When those who are on earth see the antichrist carry out the deeds prophesied in Daniel 8 (as well as Matthew 24:15-16 and 2 Thessalonians 2:4), they will know that they are in the tribulation!

"If you, my friend of the future, are wondering if that guy who has suddenly shown up on the world stage is the antichrist, then chances are the answer is yes...

"But there is still hope for you...You...can change your eternity now. You can see the antichrist for who he is, and you can see the real Christ for who He is. Give your heart to Jesus Christ while there is still time. Believe me, He is ready to give you eternal life."

Has the Tribulation Begun?, pages 173-174

TURNING OUR KNOWLEDGE INTO ACTION

If you're a believer, what should the knowledge that the tribulation is drawing near compel you to do with regard to unbelieving loved ones, friends, and others?

Below, list two or three people you know who need Christ. What specific ways can you lovingly and graciously let them know your concerns about their eternal destiny? Write your ideas here, and begin praying regularly for the Lord to open doors of ministry opportunity to you.

If you're an unbeliever, is one of the reasons you've put off repenting of your sins and receiving Christ as your Savior and Lord because you don't want to give up certain pleasures in your life?

Procrastinating a decision in the hopes you'll have time to change your mind later is never a good idea. Hebrews 9:27

says, "It is appointed for men to die once, but after this the judgment." No one knows how much time they have left, which is why 2 Corinthians 6:2 says, "Now is the day of salvation." My prayer is that you'll realize that the pleasures of heaven far exceed the pleasures of this world, and that you'll believe while there is still time.

10

A PLACE TO
CALL HOME

One way we know just how much God desires to be with His people is the fact that, in eternity, He will dwell with them forever. Revelation 21:3 says of heaven, "Behold, the tabernacle of God is with men, and He will dwell with them, and they shall be His people. God Himself will be with them and be their God." That's how much God loves those who are His own.

But for now, the fact we live in a fallen world is what keeps God separated from His creation. That separation began in the Garden of Eden, when Adam and Eve chose to rebel against God.

After the Israelites left Egypt, when they were wandering in the wilderness, God gave them instructions for building a tabernacle. Through this structure, He would dwell among His people. During the reign of King Solomon, the temporary tabernacle was replaced with a more permanent temple.

In time, however, the people's persistent rebellions against God led Him to depart from the temple.

In ancient Israel, there were two temples in Jerusalem. Both were destroyed—the first in 586 BC by King Nebuchadnezzar of Babylon, and the second in AD 70 by the armies of Rome. Today, the Temple Mount has Muslim structures on it, including the Dome of the Rock.

> "Once the church is removed from earth, the temple will be rebuilt. In fact, two temples will be built post-rapture. As the church, we will not be around to see the one, but we will worship God and celebrate our Savior at the other.
>
> "Right now, there is not a temple in Jerusalem, but one is coming. If you see a temple in Jerusalem, you are definitely in the tribulation."
>
> *Has the Tribulation Begun?*, pages 175-176

GOD WANTS TO DWELL WITH HIS CREATION

Read Genesis 3:8-10. What did Adam and Eve do after they sinned?

What punishment did God bring against Adam and Eve, according to Genesis 3:23-24?

What prideful action did mankind take against God in Genesis 11:3-4?

What did God do to prevent the people from carrying out their goal of replacing Him? (See Genesis 11:7-9.)

In Leviticus 26:11-12, what does God say that makes it clear He still desires to have a relationship with His people?

The Tabernacle—the Pre-Temple

What was the purpose of the tabernacle, according to Exodus 25:8?

Moses hungered to commune with God and pitched a tent outside the Israelite camp, and "called it the tabernacle of meeting" (Exodus 33:7). How do verses 9-11 describe the interaction that took place in this tent?

What plea did Moses make in verses 15-16?

What promise did God make in return in verse 17?

In what ways are you inspired by Moses' love and desire for interaction with God?

The First Temple—Solomon's Temple

What kind of worship was taking place in the first temple that led God to bring judgment against His people? (See Ezekiel 8:13-16.)

Read 2 Chronicles 36:15-16. When God sent messengers to warn the people to turn from their wicked ways, how did they respond?

How was the first temple destroyed, and what happened to Jerusalem, according to 2 Kings 25:8-10?

The Second Temple—Herod's Temple

After a 70-year exile in Babylon, King Cyrus of Persia declared the Jewish people could return home. It took two decades for them to rebuild the temple. How did the second temple compare to the first? (For clues, read Ezra 3:12 and Haggai 2:3.)

What did Herod the Great end up doing to the second temple? (See page 182 in *Has the Tribulation Begun?*)

What prophecy did Jesus make in John 4:21-24 about the role of the temple when it comes to worshipping God?

What does 1 Corinthians 3:16 say about the temple?

What does this mean for us?

What prophecy did Jesus give about the second temple in Matthew 24:2?

What happened to the second temple in AD 70?

The Third Temple—the Tribulation Temple

What is the identity of the prince in Daniel 8:26, and what will this prince do, according to verse 27?

What further details about this person and temple are provided for us in 2 Thessalonians 2:1-4?

Currently, the Temple Mount is in Muslim hands. How is it possible for a temple to be built on that platform? (See page 188 in *Has the Tribulation Begun?*)

What significant agreement does Daniel 9:27 say the antichrist will make with Israel?

Read Zechariah 14:4. What will eventually happen to the third temple?

The Fourth Temple—the Millennial Temple

The context of Ezekiel chapters 40–48 is the millennial kingdom. All through chapters 40–43, we see measurements and instructions given. According to Ezekiel 40:5, 41:5-6, and 43:10-12, what are these instructions for?

If this is the millennial temple, then how long can we expect it to stand? (See Revelation 20:4-6.)

God Is the Temple—Eternity

What does Revelation 21:22 tell us about the temple in eternity?

Read Revelation 21:3-6. What significant changes will we all experience in eternity?

> "God wants fellowship with His children. The Savior's desire is to abide with us, and He wants us to abide with Him. Make your decision now to take Him up on His offer of salvation as a free gift. Then you, too, can look forward to when you will walk with the Lord in the cool of the day in His new heavens and new earth."
>
> *Has the Tribulation Begun?*, page 191

TURNING OUR KNOWLEDGE INTO ACTION

If you're already a Christian, what is the state of your relationship with God right now?

In what ways do you see room for growth in your relationship with Him?

If you're an unbeliever, what are you missing by not being in relationship with God?

What does Romans 10:9-10 say about receiving Christ as your Savior and Lord?

11

WRATH ON DISPLAY

Perhaps the one aspect of the tribulation people are most curious about are the details about the judgments God will pour out upon the earth. These judgments will take part in three stages—the seven seal judgments, the seven trumpet judgments, and the seven bowl judgments. The book of Revelation provides an abundance of details about what will happen. While some people differ on how to interpret the language that describes these judgments, one fact is certain: They will be terrible in scope and intensity.

Earlier, we learned about the signs that will help us to know we are drawing closer to the Lord's coming. Here, we'll look at what will occur during the tribulation itself. When those who are alive on earth during this time see these events unfolding all around them, they will know, with certainty, that they are in the tribulation.

And they will know that time is running out for them to make a decision about their eternal destiny. As we will see, there will be many who are resolute in their rejection of God.

But there will also be a good number of people who realize the error of their ways and seek salvation in Christ.

> "The church is made up of people, wherever they may be at any given moment, who have accepted Jesus Christ as their Savior and Lord, thereby receiving the free gift of salvation that comes through Jesus' death and resurrection. If that describes you, what follows should not bring you fear, only sorrow for your unsaved loved ones and motivation to tell them how they can escape this fate. If you have not committed yourself to Christ, however, then you should be terrified, because what I am about to describe to you is constrained by the limits of the English language. The reality will be much, much worse."
>
> *Has the Tribulation Begun?*, page 193

SUPERNATURAL ACTIVITIES

What does 2 Thessalonians 2:9-10 tell us that the antichrist will be empowered to do?

Who will make this display of power possible?

What will the antichrist's right-hand person, the false prophet, be able to do, according to Revelation 13:13-14?

Both the antichrist and the false prophet will carry out deception on a massive scale. Why do you think they will be so successful in deluding people?

Read Revelation 11:3-6. What other two people will be able to do miracles during the tribulation?

What does Revelation 11:7-9 say will happen to these two miracle workers?

How will the people of the earth respond to the momentary fate of the two? (See Revelation 11:10.)

What will God then do to the two, and what calamity will occur in Jerusalem, according to Revelation 11:11-13?

While the antichrist and false prophet will perform super-natural activities to deceive people, God and His two witnesses will do the supernatural to confirm that ultimately, it is God who possesses all power and control over what happens.

Wars and Violence

Though wars and violence are a very real part of our world today, how will they differ during the tribulation?

Just how serious of a picture does Revelation 6:4 provide about what world conditions will be like on earth during the tribulation?

Read Revelation 16:14-16 and 19:19-21. How extensive will the forces be that come against Christ at the end of the tribulation?

How bad will the carnage be, according to Zechariah 14:12-15 and Revelation 19:17-18?

Scarcity and Economic Collapse

What will happen when the third seal judgment is unleashed? (See Revelation 6:5-6.)

Imagine a truly global economic collapse taking place. What effects do you think that would have on people?

Death

Read Revelation 6:7-8. How much of the earth's population will be killed when the fourth seal judgment occurs?

How many more people will be killed when the sixth trumpet judgment takes place? (See Revelation 9:18.)

Considering how many will be killed during the tribulation, what are some difficulties you think people will face with so many deaths in such a short period of time?

Diseases

Read Revelation 6:7-8. What will happen to one-fourth of the earth when the fourth seal judgment occurs?

What affliction is described in Revelation 16:2?

Earthquakes

In Revelation 6:12-14, what are we told about the effects of the "great earthquake" that will make it stand out from the earthquakes we experience today?

What will accompany the earthquake mentioned in Revelation 11:19?

What clue is given about the severity of the earthquake described in Revelation 16:18-19?

Things Falling from the Skies

Read Revelation 8:7-10. Has anything ever occurred on Earth that comes even close to what is described here? What do you think some of the serious side effects will be of these disasters?

When the second and third bowl judgments take place, as described in Revelation 8:10-11, what will happen to the waters on Earth?

What are some results that are likely to occur due to a lack of fresh water?

Contrasting Calamities

According to Revelation 16:8-9, what will happen on Earth when the fourth bowl judgment is poured out?

And what will take place when the fourth trumpet judgment sounds? (See Revelation 8:12.)

FINAL WORDS

In response to all the judgments we've read about, how will most of the people on Earth respond?

Revelation 6:16—

Revelation 9:6—

Revelation 16:11—

At the same time, we are informed that many will become saved during the tribulation. Read Revelation 7:9-10. What does the apostle John see?

According to verse 14, where did these people come from?

Though it is true that people will become saved during the tribulation, you absolutely do not want to put off receiving salvation in Christ until then. As we've already seen, billions of people will die, and many others will still reject God even though they know it is He who is pouring out the judgments.

As Paul wrote in 2 Corinthians 6:2, "Behold, now is the accepted time; behold, now is the day of salvation." You never know what tomorrow might bring, or how much time you might have left.

> "Humanity's rebellion against its Creator deserves every ounce of the coming wrath. But God's desire is that no one experience the tribulation. In fact, He wanted so much to spare you from it that Jesus subjected Himself to suffering, torture,

and a horrifically violent death just so you could be spared the punishment of your sin. Do not let His sacrifice for you go to waste. Do not open yourself up to the suffering of the tribulation. Choose salvation. Choose hope. Choose Jesus."

Has the Tribulation Begun?, page 205

TURNING OUR KNOWLEDGE INTO ACTION

What did Christ endure to spare people of the punishment they deserve for their sins?

If you are a believer, what is an appropriate response to the sacrifice Christ made on your behalf?

If you are an unbeliever, would you agree the extent of Christ's suffering for your sake is confirmation of how much He loves you?

1:2

WHAT'S MOST IMPORTANT

Reading about the end times is sobering. As we consider the judgments that will take place, we come to realize the seriousness of sin. When unbelievers choose to rebel against God, they're saying they want nothing to do with Him. In making that choice, they also choose their eternal destination.

Prophecies about the end times are sobering in another way as well. For believers, they are a wake-up call to the fact time is short. At the same time that Scripture teaches us about the nearness of Christ's coming, it also admonishes us to live in an ongoing state of readiness.

What does living in constant anticipation of the rapture look like? How does it affect our life choices and priorities? You may know Christians who are so focused on the end times that they aren't fully engaged in opportunities God has given them for the present moment. More likely, you know believers who are so caught up in the here and now that they aren't living with the future in mind. They don't have an eternal perspective.

As we close out this study guide, let's learn what it means to live with an eternal perspective and, at the same time, actively live out Christ's commands for the day-to-day aspect of our lives.

> "So, has the tribulation begun? No, it has not. However, by all indications, it is not far away. But even more important than the fact of God's impending wrath drawing ever nearer is the question, 'So what?' If I knew that the rapture was going to take place tomorrow or next year or a decade from now, how should I live my life today? And should the primary focus of my life be any different based on a tomorrow rapture compared to a 2032 departure?"
>
> *Has the Tribulation Begun?*, page 207

THE BELIEVER'S CONTRADICTION

On page 207 of *Has the Tribulation Begun?*, we read, "For the Christian, life on this earth is a continuous contradiction." What is this contradiction?

What are some of the temporal things that believers can easily be distracted by?

What are some of our eternal priorities?

Why do we sometimes have difficulty living out those priorities?

In Hebrews chapter 11, we read about great people of the Bible whom God worked through. Carefully read verses 13-16. How did they view themselves in relation to earth, according to verse 13?

What does verse 16 say they desired?

What exhortation does the apostle Paul give us in Colossians 3:1-2?

What is our mission, as stated in Matthew 28:18-20?

On page 209 of *Has the Tribulation Begun?*, we read, "We must be constantly on the job, always looking for those who need to know the truth." What does this look like for you in your unique life situation? For example, you may be a parent of schoolchildren, a workplace employee, and a neighbor. Given your current place in life, how can you be constantly on the job?

On pages 209-210 of *Has the Tribulation Begun?*, we read, "When it comes down to it, the disciples were no different than you or me." Why is this the case? Try to think of two or three reasons.

Mission over Comfort

The vast majority of believers in the Western world don't experience true persecution. What is the worst we're likely to face?

Why should these obstacles not bother us when it comes to sharing our faith? (In your answer, consider the worst we have to lose, versus the best of what we have to gain.)

Read Ephesians 2:8-10. What responsibility does verse 10 call us to?

On page 211 of *Has the Tribulation Begun?*, we read, "When we say yes to Jesus, we are not just becoming part of His family, we are joining up with His workforce." Because of where God has placed you, what are you uniquely able to do for His kingdom that others might not be able to do?

You might not have a large or recognized ministry, but it's not the size or prominence of your ministry that counts. What do you think counts most to the Lord?

In Matthew 16:24-25, how costly did Jesus say it would be to follow Him?

How are you doing when it comes to sacrificing your comfort in pursuit of your calling?

Unity over Division

What are some examples of nondoctrinal and comparatively insignificant issues that Christians easily become divided over?

What cultural factors do you think are contributing to the increased division in today's church?

Do you think it is possible for two Christians who disagree

politically to still experience true unity spiritually and in other ways? Why should that be possible?

What are two or three ways you or someone you know has experienced petty division? How do you think God views such division?

What command did Jesus give in John 13:34-35, and most importantly, why?

How can we do a better job of discerning between the essentials of the faith and nonessentials so that we can know more unity with our fellow believers?

Christ over Everything Else

The best way you can fulfill your mission here on earth is by being an ambassador for Christ. Below, list the different avenues you have available to you to be an ambassador for our Lord.

What do the following passages say about being an ambassador?

Matthew 5:13-14—

Philippians 2:14—

Romans 12:14-21—

For the last passage above, what areas would you like to improve upon in your own life?

NOW IS THE TIME

In light of what you've learned in this lesson, what are some prayer requests you can lift up to the Lord as you ask Him to make you a better ambassador? List them here.

"The window of opportunity to escape the coming tribulation is closing. Don't let anything distract you from readying yourself or from letting your loved ones know that now is the time to grab the oil. Now is the time to prepare your heart."

Has the Tribulation Begun?, page 216

TURNING OUR KNOWLEDGE INTO ACTION

Paul wrote, "I have fought the good fight, I have finished the race, I have kept the faith" (2 Timothy 4:7). As you look at your life now, in what two or three areas do you see the greatest need for growth so that you can echo Paul's words?

What attitudes do you think are important for you to cultivate so that you, too, can be diligent and persevere in your service to the Lord?

Take some time now to pray and ask the Lord to help guide you as you seek to be a better ambassador for Him.

OTHER GREAT HARVEST HOUSE
BOOKS BY AMIR TSARFATI

Amir Tsarfati, with Dr. Rick Yohn, examines what Revelation makes known about the end times and beyond. Guided by accessible teaching that lets Scripture speak for itself, you'll see what lies ahead for every person in the end times—either in heaven or on earth. Are *you* ready?

This companion workbook to *Revealing Revelation*—the product of many years of careful research—offers you a clear and exciting overview of God's perfect plan for the future. Inside you'll find principles from the Bible that equip you to better interpret the end-times signs, as well as insights about how Bible prophecy is relevant to your life today.

In *Israel and the Church*, bestselling author and native Israeli Amir Tsarfati helps readers recognize the distinct contemporary and future roles of both the Jewish people and the church, and how together they reveal the character of God and His perfect plan of salvation.

To fully grasp what God has in store for the future, it's vital to understand His promises to Israel. The *Israel and the Church Study Guide* will help you do exactly that, equipping you to explore the Bible's many revelations about what is yet to come.

As a native Israeli of Jewish roots, Amir Tsarfati provides a distinct perspective that weaves biblical history, current events, and Bible prophecy together to shine light on the mysteries about the end times. In *The Day Approaching*, he points to the scriptural evidence that the return of the Lord is imminent.

Jesus Himself revealed the signs that will alert us to the nearness of His return. In *The Day Approaching Study Guide*, you'll have the opportunity to take an up-close look at what those signs are, as well as God's overarching plans for the future, and how those plans affect you today.

AMIR TSARFATI WITH BARRY STAGNER

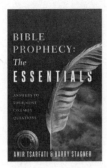

In *Bible Prophecy: The Essentials*, Amir and Barry team up to answer 70 of their most commonly asked questions. Through succinct, Scripture-focused teachings, Amir and Barry address seven foundational themes of Bible prophecy: Israel, the church, the rapture, the tribulation, the millennium, the Great White Throne judgment, and heaven.

AMIR TSARFATI WITH STEVE YOHN

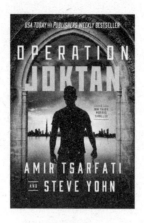

BOOK 1

"It was the perfect day—until the gunfire."

Nir Tavor is an Israeli secret service operative turned talented Mossad agent.

Nicole le Roux is a model with a hidden skill.

A terrorist attack brings them together, and then work forces them apart—until they're unexpectedly called back into each other's lives.

But there's no time for romance. As violent radicals threaten chaos across the Middle East, the two must work together to stop these extremists, pooling Nicole's knack for technology and Nir's adeptness with on-the-ground missions. Each heart-racing step of their operation gets them closer to the truth—and closer to danger.

In this thrilling first book in a new series, authors Amir Tsarfati and Steve Yohn draw on true events as well as tactical insights Amir learned from his time in the Israeli Defense Forces. For believers in God's life-changing promises, *Operation Joktan* is a suspense-filled page-turner that illuminates the blessing Israel is to the world.

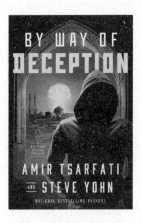

BOOK 2

The Mossad has uncovered Iran's plans to smuggle untraceable weapons of mass destruction into Israel. The clock is ticking, and agents Nir Tavor and Nicole le Roux can't act quickly enough.

Nir and Nicole find themselves caught in a whirlwind plot of assassinations, espionage, and undercover recon, fighting against the clock to stop this threat against the Middle East. As they draw closer to danger—and closer to each other—they find themselves ensnared in a lethal web of secrets. Will they have to sacrifice their own lives to protect the lives of millions?

Inspired by real events, authors Amir Tsarfati and Steve Yohn reteam for this suspenseful follow-up to the bestselling *Operation Joktan*. Filled with danger, romance, and international intrigue, this Nir Tavor thriller reveals breathtaking true insights into the lives and duties of Mossad agents—and delivers a story that will have you on the edge of your seat.